In case you haven't met him yet, this is the real **Winston!**
He's a lovely, kind, and sweet Boston Terrier dog who has been an incredible friend to my family. He's so special that I wanted to create this book series with my dad, turning him into a genius superhero on a mission to save the universe! Thank you so much for supporting us and picking up the second book in our series!

Love Mia Age 7 ❤

Colin, Sarah, and of course Winston!

To My Amazing Mia...
Some of my best memories were the times we spent together, watching you grow up, storyboarding, scheming and building these books with your incredible imagination. Don't stop Dreaming!
Love you forever!
Dad...

Previously, Beneath
The Bone Shop...

Winston, the superhero of our story, along with Teddy and his super-hyperactive dad Diesel, discovered something huge. A secret maze of twisting magical tunnels, built by mysterious beings with secrets older than time. The tunnels are filled with traps, puzzles, enemies and their robots that are desperate to steal Winston's Cosmic Bone. Armed with Winston's trusty backpack full of tiny nanotech machines that transform into all kinds of sporty gadgets, and the amazing Cosmic Bone that can shape-shift, decode languages, and help Winston outsmart any enemy. Now they continue on their journey to a section where some unique creatures are protecting a very special door. "Winston, my mate! They have ears just like you!" woofed Diesel in amazement as they all laughed at the similarity.

It was none other than a family of watchful, magical rabbits! "Greetings, adventurers," Sir Fluffles III (the 3rd) warmly welcomed them, his voice both calm and wise. "We are the creators and guardians of the great tunnel systems. For thousands of years, our families have built and watched over them, protecting the secrets within. To pass, you must answer two of our trickiest riddles."

1. What is bright orange, topped with green, and sounds like a word for some talking birds?

2. I have cities with no houses. I have mountains with no trees. I have paths with no roads. What am I?

Winston solved every riddle like a pro. The rabbits cheered as the magical door vanished. They then shared carrots together and, using their secretive map, guided the adventurers through the maze to the final challenge.

1. CARROT 2. MAP

Megaflop Galaxy System

Meanwhile, far across the cosmos, Disco Duck, the leader of the Claw Crew, was busy plotting his next big plan to outsmart Winston! Disco Duck was a truly funny and very quirky duck who was seriously passionate about 80's dance music, milk, and insisted on having disco balls in every single corner of his gigantic spaceship. He'd made the air and gravity just right inside his spaceship so he could still dance, and his milk drops could float around without boiling. With his clever inventions, powerful robotic drones, and a team of loyal secret agents, he was a big deal all over the galaxy!

Spy Club Fact
Liquids do some super weird things in space! Outside of the spaceship, liquids would boil then freeze solid into tiny ice crystals due to the lack of any air pressure. Brrr!

A few moments earlier, some really bad news appeared on Disco Duck's control screens from Planet Earth. One of his top agents, Smokestrike, the mysterious black ninja cat, was still stuck in Winston's super sticky bubble gum trap in the tunnels beneath the bone shop! "Seriously? I can't believe we have to rescue that silly cat again! What is wrong with him?" Disco Duck quacked.

"What do we have to do to get that Cosmic Bone?" He shook his head in disbelief.
"Enough of this nonsense! I'm a super evil genius, not a pet rescuer!" Then he paused, busted a move on the dance floor as the rainbow lights from his disco ball swirled around him, and quacked, "It's time for a plan so brilliant, Winston won't know what hit him!"

Disco Duck quacked orders to his robot drone, "Quacker, stop waddling about! Grab the Time Twister TT427B, jump to an earlier time, and stop Smokestrike from getting into that bubblegum mess! And don't forget to tell agent Smokestrike that Winston's weakness is his eyesight. He needs to break Winston's glasses first, then send him as far back in time as possible so he can't mess up our plans again!" Quacker replied, "Project Free Smokey is a go, Captain Disco! Quack! Quack!" Little did they know, a very special visitor had just sneaked onto their spaceship and was about to slip through the portal without being seen.

The Timetwister can bend interdimensional time, and is capable of opening portals to any time and place in the universe!

Chaos Unleashed

Sad Face is a super grumpy, shape-shifting yellow octopus known across the galaxy for his amazing machine-building skills. One of his early time machines went wrong and scattered his family and friends across the universe. For centuries, he has worked as a space engineer on the pinkish silver planet known as Rhodium. Where he has been trying to replicate the Claw Crew's Time Twister device to travel through time to find them. Sad Face loves creating TV shows, watching fast action films, loud rock music, collecting gold and funny bumper stickers. If you look closely at his spaceship, you might see some of them! Even though he grumbles a lot and causes trouble throughout the universe. He is really just lonely and wants some attention. Sadly for him, no one likes hanging out with super grumpy alien octopuses.

Spy Club Fact

Rhodium, in case you are wondering, is a pinkish silver metal that is more valuable than gold here on Earth. It's part of the platinum group of metals.

Sad Face was very adaptable, much like the octopuses here on Earth. He could squeeze into tight spaces, climb any surface, and even change how he looks. Interestingly, he has built his spaceship to change size and even hide itself with its cloaking technology.

As Disco Duck's drones powered up the Time Twister, Sad Face spotted an opportunity and slipped through the time portal without being seen, ready for a new adventure to cause chaos on a very special planet called Earth.

Spy Club Search Try spotting Sad Face through the story as he is now using his invisibility tech to remain hidden.

Within the depths of the labyrinth, Winston, Teddy, and his super-energetic father, Diesel, moved cautiously through the tunnels. Soon, they came across a dark, eerie cave. Hanging over a massive chasm was a shaky, ancient bridge. "A swing bridge!" Diesel shouted excitedly. "These are the best!" Without a second thought, he rushed onto the bridge, eager to cross and test it out. Suddenly, a loud crack echoed through the tunnels. Before anyone could react, Diesel and the bridge started to fall into the darkness below!

NOO!

AW! no?

Crackk!

Spy Club Challenge Which sporting equipment would you activate to get to Diesel the quickest?

Hang Glider   Bungee Cord   Jetpack   Grappling Hook

"Nooo!" Teddy howled as Winston plunged into the abyss after his friend. As the nanobots from his bag whirred and transformed into a super-fast jetpack, he shot across the chasm at tremendous speed to reach Diesel in time and collect Teddy, delivering them both safely to the other side of the broken bridge. Diesel, his voice thick with an Australian accent, shouted, "Thanks for the save, ya little flippin' ripper! That was a close one, eh? Yeah! I thought I was a goner for sure!" Teddy's voice brimmed with frustration. "Dad, you have to stop rushing ahead! This place is really dangerous!"

Winston grinned and said, 'No stress, Diesel. We're just chuffed you're still here. But let's be real guys, my tummy sounds like a lion that has been eating vegetables for two weeks after all that excitement!' Teddy, ever prepared, grabbed a handful of his delicious dog treats from his shop and tossed them into the air for Winston.

Slobber-Licious Biscuits, Woof-tastic Chews and Barky Bones filled the air with a variety of delicious flavours, as they all headed straight for Winston's mouth. "Teddy, your snacks are really something special, hey! Truly amazing!", he replied in sheer awe as he gobbled all the delicious treats.

Final Challenge

The next cave featured four stone statues representing fire, water, time and earth. Large ancient text was illuminating from the wall in front of them that Winston translated...

In the heart of this room,
your final challenge awaits.
Listen with care, as the riddle begins...

I have no beginning. I have no end.
I am always present, and always will be.
Press down on my correct statue.

Time

Diesel jumped without discussing it with his team and pressed down on the time stone. Suddenly, a bright flash of light filled the room, and the floor beneath them spun and swirled. Before they could even catch their breath, they were tumbling head over paws into a giant, swirling ancient super-tube. They whooshed through dark tunnels, zooming past glowing rocks and sparkling waterfalls. At last, with a big splash, they all crash landed into a hidden underground lake.

Teddy opened his eyes and saw his dad and Winston both grinning at him. "Good on ya, Dad. You absolutely nailed that riddle! But next time, maybe just wait for us, yeah?"

"I did it again, sorry fellas... Will definitely have to practice my patience and give you lot a heads-up next time," he chuckled. "Wouldn't want ya guys to miss out on all the fun!"

The Orbs

Six glowing orbs floated on the water, holding within them a kaleidoscope of shimmering and dancing lights. "They look magical, like they're alive!" exclaimed Teddy. Suddenly, Quasar appeared once more. "Well done, adventurers!

You have shown great courage and never gave up. You have completed all our ancient challenges and are worthy to wield the elemental Orbs." Quasar's voice was warm and kind. "These orbs will choose the superheroes who are ready to unleash their powers."

Spy Club Power-Up — Which orb superpowers would you pick, and how would you defend Earth?

Fire Orb, with its ability to generate and control heat and flame.

Water Orb has the power to control water, snow, ice, and steam.

Light Orb holds the power of light, speed, invisibility and healing.

Air Orb allows the user to alter the air density, to move objects, control the weather and even fly.

Earth Orb rumbles with the strength of the ground, allowing the control of both plants and earth.

Realm Orb unlocks portals to any timeline and realities, allowing the user to explore new worlds.

Diesel's eyes sparkled as he exclaimed, "No way, we're going to be flippen superdogs mate! I was not expecting that! How about we call ourselves the Slobber Squad, fellas?" Diesel barked, his tail wagging with excitement. "Great name, Dad! Let's see what they can do first!" Teddy replied.

As the heroes stepped closer to the glowing orbs, a strange energy buzzed through the air. Quasar chuckled, "By the way, heroes, it looks like some of your enemies are coming. Good luck! I'll be watching all the action!"

"ENEMIES? What could be coming for us now?" Teddy whimpered. Winston's face showed pure excitement for whatever was about to jump at them from the shadows. "Aweh, my bru! This is it! Get ready...", Winston woofed.

Spy Club Slang

In case you are wondering... "Aweh" is exclamation of excitement, and "bru" is short for brother or friend in South African slang.

Ninja Attack

Suddenly someone incredibly sneeky tripped Winston and made his glasses fly through the air... Smokestrike whipped out his razor-sharp ninja sword and sliced the glasses clean in half as he reached out to steal the Cosmic Bone. The Claw Crew's Quacker Robot quickly twisted the Time Twister's dial to 68 million BC as the robot reached for the activation switch.

"Hahahaha! Enjoy the dinosaur era, Winston. No one will be able to save you this time!" Smokestrike hissed.

ANCIENT EGYPT
51 BC

NOO!

After losing his vision, Winston felt a surge of powerful energy building inside the Time Twister. Suddenly, the image of a gigantic disco ball flashed into his mind. In that instant, the Cosmic Bone responded, transforming into a shimmering, reflective shield that enveloped Teddy, Diesel, and Winston that pushed Smokestrike right back.

The Time Twister's blast exploded in every direction as it collided with the Disco Ball, sending ripples of power through the very fabric of space and time. The impact with the Cosmic Bone seemed to alter the dates, and hurled Winston along with Sad Face, who had been silently hidden this whole time to the year 51 BC into the heart of ancient Egypt, during the reign of Queen Cleopatra's rule.

Another time portal shot out for 68 million BC, hurling Smokestrike the naughty cat ninja towards the age of dinosaurs as the disco ball shield disappeared! Miraculously untouched by the blast, Teddy and Diesel huddled together next to Disco Duck's broken Quacker Robot. Confused and unsure what to do next, they started wondering where Winston disappeared to and how they could save him with the new, mysterious orbs that lay in front of them.

HSSS!

JURASSIC ERA
68,000,000 BC

The Age Of Dinosaurs

The naughty Smokestrike was instantly teleported millions of years back to one of the scariest periods imaginable, when enormous dinosaurs roamed the Earth.

Spy Club Fact

Lucky for Smokestrike here the **Diplodocus** was a vegetarian, so it was only interrested in plants. It did however have a powerful large whip like tail that could scare away hungry predators.

Within seconds of Smokestrike arriving, every predator in the area seemed to know that an incredibly new tasty snack had just appeared in their world. Smokestrike looked around, his eyes wide with fear. He saw towering trees, strange plants, and giant bugs all around him. Then, there was a roar in the distance that could have only been a huge terrifying T-Rex that was coming right towards him! "Uh oh. That definitely doesn't sound friendly." Smokestrike gulped as he started to run as fast as he possibly could. Suddenly the ground shook as the T-Rex shot out from the forest and charged the little Ninja cat!

Tyrannosaurus rex (T. Rex) roamed the Earth during the Late Cretaceous period, approximately 66 to 68 million years ago, near the end of the Mesozoic Era, often called the "Age of Dinosaurs." Smokestrike was pleasantly surprised to learn how slow the mighty T. rex was, estimating its speed at only 12-19 km/h—far slower than the average cat, which can sprint at an impressive 48 km/h!

Smokestrike raced through the thick prehistoric jungle, his heart pounding like a war drum. Behind him, the snarls and thunderous footfalls of ravenous predators closed in fast. Strange plants lashed at his face as he sprinted, but he didn't flinch. Survival was his only goal. Up ahead, a cluster of towering trees broke through the misty canopy. In one fluid motion, he pulled out a smoke bomb from his ninja suit, and hurled it to the forest floor. A blast of dark vapour erupted behind him as he launched into the air in a daring upward leap. Moments later, he vanished into the tangle of treetops above.

Smokestrike paused high in the treetops, catching his breath as the sounds of pursuit faded below. For a moment, he thought he was safe. He let out a quiet sigh of relief. Then everything changed... Massive shadows swept across the canopy. He looked up just as a piercing screech ripped through the sky. A monstrous pteranodon, its ember-toned wings stretched wide, came diving straight toward him, slicing through the air with terrifying speed. In an instant, Smokestrike held on upside down underneath one of the large branches as leaves scattered in its wake as the huge creature flew past.

Pssssst...
Don't worry about Smokestrike!
He is a ninja cat, after all!
Meanwhile lets see how
Sad Face and Winston are doing
back in Ancient Egypt 51 BC.

Ancient Egypt : 51 BC

As Winston and Sad Face landed in ancient Egypt, Winston squinted at the swirling lights around him. Everything was blurry, as he couldn't see a thing without his glasses. He pressed a button on his bag again and again. But instead of making a new pair of glasses, it just made things worse! First, it built a pair of night-vision goggles that turned everything a spooky, glowing green. Then came some diving goggles! "These are not helpful at all!" Winston groaned. He quickly turned the dial on his bag to sunglasses with special lenses. The nanobots instantly buzzed across his face as a perfect pair of sunglasses appeared. Everything snapped into focus as he could now see and hear someone incredibly grumpy behind him.

SERIOUSLY?

"Sad Face!? **Haibo...** What are you doing here?" Winston barked, his tail stiff in shock. "Urgh, I was following the Time Twister, until your silly space bone sent us to boiling hot ancient Egypt of all places?! It feels like... **I'm melting here!**" the alien moaned, as his skin glowed bright **red** in anger. Winston stared in amazement at the Great Pyramids, standing tall and proud in their original glory while his tummy gave a very loud rumble, reminding him of his hunger after their long journey through time.

Spy Club Slang

"Haibo" is a common word widely used in South African English from the Zulu language that is used to express shock, surprise, disbelief or emotion. **Try it!**

Suddenly Sad Face spotted something on the otherside of the Nile River that was about to change everything. The broken Claw Crew's Time Twister device had somehow come into the ancient Egyptian timeline. "Ooo, what a perfect situation!" he exclaimed, jittery with excitement. Without wasting a second, he grabbed the device and scrambled into his super cooled, sleek spaceship. The door shut quietly, and without making a sound, the ship shot up into the sky and disappeared in a split second. Winston's heart raced. "Eish, no! This can't be happening... My hungry stomach distracted me again!" he whispered. "If he fixes that Time Twister device, he could smash the whole universe into bits, and it's my fault!

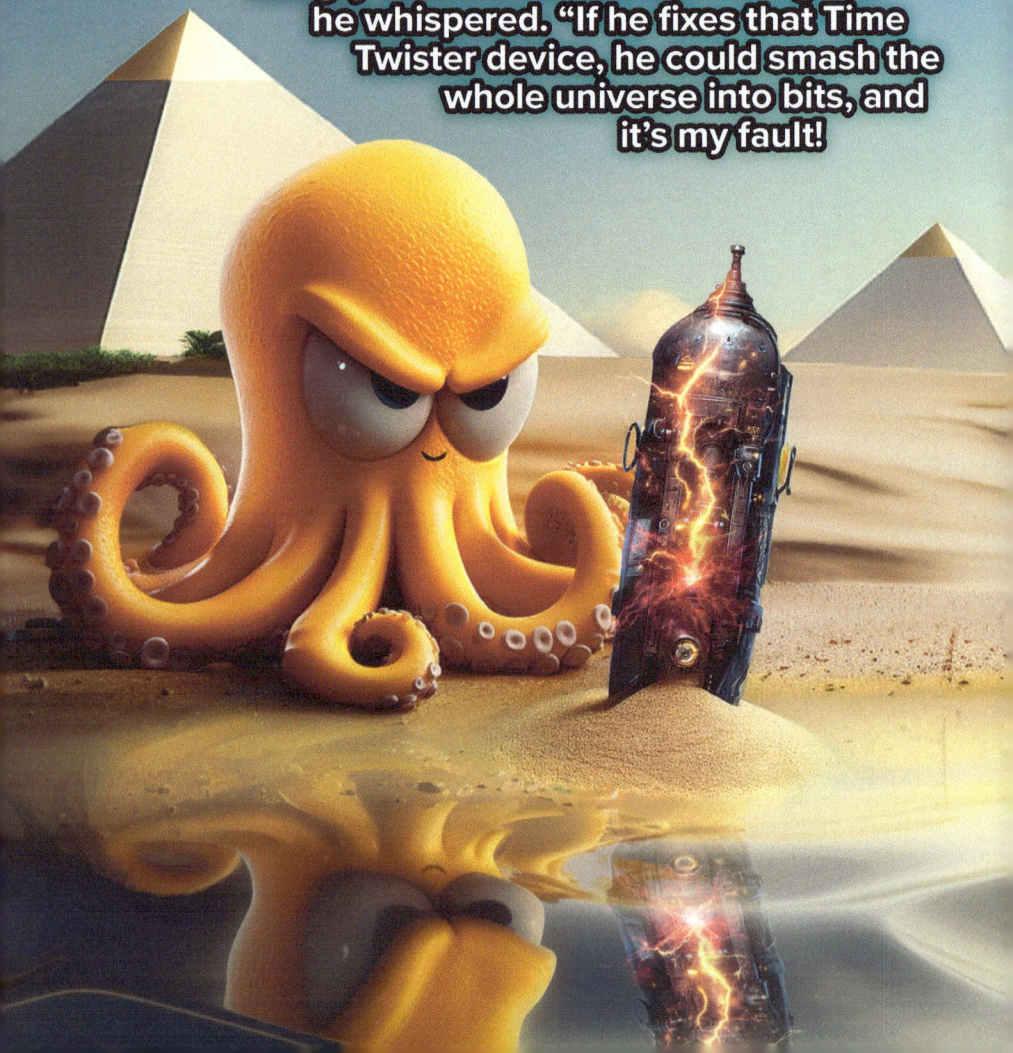

Sad Face sped off to the Valley of the Kings, where ancient Egyptian pharaohs were buried with their treasures. There he gathered as much gold and silver as he could carry. Then buried all his stolen artefacts deep beneath the sandy riverbed of the Nile River. He smiled, knowing that no one would find it for thousands of years.

Spy Club Search

Try to find the gold statues. How many can you count?

Finding Cleopatra

Sad Face was now solely focused on replicating and making the new Time Twister blaster more dangerous in his laboratory by increasing the size of the portals. If he succeeded, the consequences would be catastrophic. Winston's mission was to recruit Queen Cleopatra, the most powerful cat in all of Egypt, which meant finding her in her heavily guarded palace was going to be a challenge.

Spy Club Challenge

Which sporting equipment would you activate to get past Cleopatra's guards?

Trampoline
Bouncy Blaster

Bowling Ball
Gutterballer

Basketball
Court Crusher

Skateboard
Frictionless Flyer

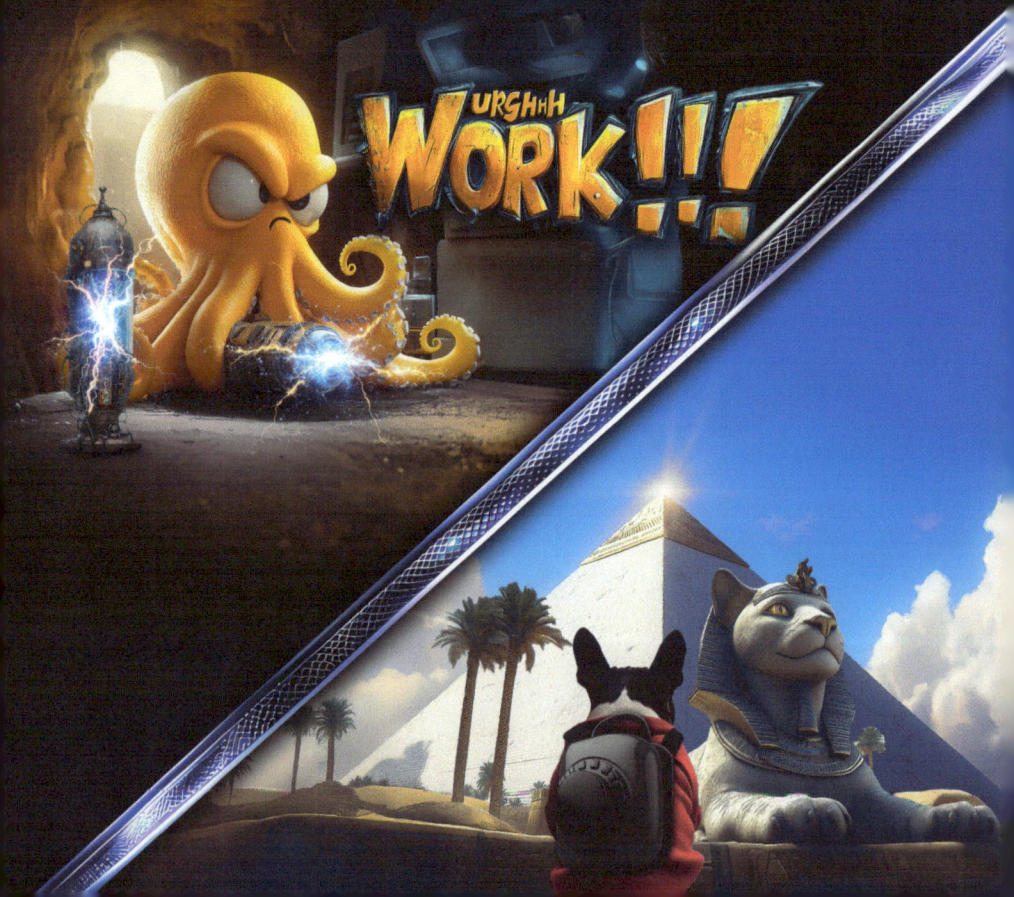

Cosmic Slam Dunk

Winston turned on his jet-powered glider as his sunglasses changed into a new pair of flying goggles as he soared high above ancient Egypt. The pyramids and temples below sparkled in the golden sunlight. He spotted Cleopatra's palace in the distance and knew it would be hard to get inside with so many guards. Then an idea popped into his head, as he threw his Cosmic Bone into the air and cut his engine. He then pictured himself inside a giant basketball.

In an instant, the Cosmic Bone transformed into a springy orange sphere around him that rocketed towards the palace doors at incredible speed.

Winston zoomed through the air towards Cleopatra's palace. The giant orange basketball blasted through the front gates, bouncing and crashing past statues and the Queen's guards before coming to a sudden stop in front of her throne. One of her brave guards immediately stepped forward and, with a powerful thrust, punctured the rubber ball with his spear. The ball deflated with a loud hiss, as Winston rolled right up to the great Queen.

Her voice rang out in ancient Greek. "Who are you? Explain yourself this instant!" she hissed. "I've come with an urgent message, Queen Cleopatra," Winston replied in perfect Greek, thanks to the power of the Cosmic Bone. "A grumpy alien octopus called Sad Face has come here from the future with a machine that can twist time. If we don't stop him, he could put the whole universe in danger!"

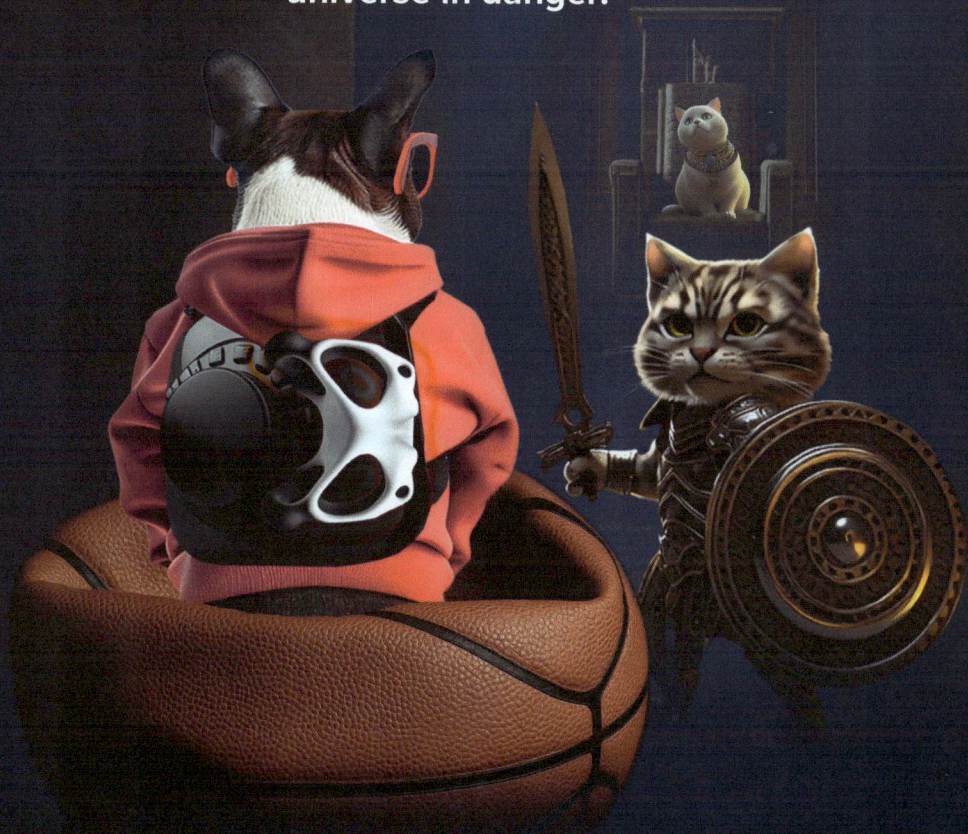

🐾 Spy Club Fact

Did you know... Queen Cleopatra wasn't Egyptian! She was actually Greek and a descendant of Ptolemy, one of Alexander the Great's generals.

Cleopatra's face changed. She quickly walked outside and asked Winston to follow her. The view of the pyramids and the Nile River were amazing. She was no longer angry. Instead, she looked very curious and a little worried. "I believe you, Winston the Titan," she said. "You speak of danger and an enemy we have never seen before. My army will help you. But how can we stop a strange alien octopus when his weapons are far ahead of anything we have at this period in time?", Cleopatra replied.

"We need to find the biggest, shiniest objects your army can find! We can stick them in the sand and bounce the time-blasts right back at Sad Face." he exclaimed his eyes wide with excitement.

Suddenly he got incredibly distracted as his eyes widened. "Wait a second... It can't be! Is that BILTONG?!" he gasped, watching in awe as his best snack was brought in front of them!

"It's just dried meat, Winston. We have tons of it! Drying out meat is how we prevent our food from spoiling and is great for long term storage. We've never heard of Biltong before. Is that what you call it in the future?"

"They sure do, especially from my neck of the woods, in sunny South Africa!" Winston replied as he happily munched away. Cleopatra then quickly turned to her soldiers. "Bring the shiniest shields in all of Egypt!" she shouted. "Today, we will save Egypt!"

The Master Plan

Even though Sad Face had stolen all the treasure in Egypt and fixed the Time Twister, he still just couldn't stop moaning. "This heat is the worst!" he grumbled. "It feels like my brain is turning into space goo. How does anyone live here? My tentacles are cooking!" He slithered into his spaceship and pressed a button on the control panel as the Time Twister began to glow. "Finally now that everything's working..." he smirked. "All I need is some cold air and a bit of prehistoric fun to liven things up!"

Sad Face's real plan was far worse than anyone could have imagined. He didn't just want to fix the Time Twister. He wanted to make time portals large enough to transport destructive creatures from other timelines! Why? So he could film all the chaos and turn it into a new show called **Intergalactic Wars!**

Sad Face wriggled his tentacles with excitement. He could already picture himself becoming famous, with dinosaurs destroying Egypt. He jumped into his spaceship and zoomed through a portal back to **68 million BC.**

When he arrived, he didn't just see one dinosaur… there were hundreds of them! And running right towards Sad Face's spaceship was none other than Smokestrike!

"Urghh, what is that fluffy pest doing here?!" Sad Face groaned. "I hate hitchhikers! Now I'm going to have to vacuum up all his cat fluff all over the place! Urghhh! Hmm, I suppose he might become quite useful as dinosaur bait… they do really seem to love him!"

Sad Face quickly flicked the Time Twister button, that opened a swirling time portal for the rampaging dinosaurs, then opened the spaceship's hatch for Smokestrike! **The Chaos King.**

AREA 51

Smokestrike sprang into action, launching into a whirlwind of cartwheels and somersaults before rocketing himself safely into Sad Face's spaceship.

In seconds, a thundering herd of dinosaurs charged straight through the portal into Ancient Egypt! Out of nowhere, a massive T. Rex stomped forward behind them as it chomped down and swallowed Sad Face's spaceship whole.

Gone! Just like that...
as they both descended into the dark belly of one of the largest meat-eating dinosaurs in history.

Inside the T-Rex's Belly

"BLARGH! Silly Cat!" Sad Face shouted, turning bright red with rage. "How does this sort of stuff only happen when you are around?" Smokestrike flicked his tail and rolled his eyes in frustration. "Hey! I didn't choose to get chased by a bunch of super hungry dinosaurs!" he snapped. "You wouldn't have lasted two seconds outside of this calamari can!"

"Well, I guess it's time to improvise! Welcome to the party fluffy." Sad Face said with a sly grin. He then hit the ROCK button on his spaceship's control panel. Suddenly rock music blasted so loudly through the whole of the T-Rex's body, which caused the giant dinosaur to break out into some hilariously wild dance moves. With a thunderous, musical roarrr, the T-Rex spat the spaceship out, launching it flying through the jungle.

"Get off me already, silly cat! Can you stop breathing so loudly?" Sad Face complained. Smokestrike's cat hair made him sneeze so much that snot went flying all over his tiny spaceship! Grumbling, he continued to steer toward a distant marker on his map. "Hey, Captain Calamari, you're going the wrong way," Smokestrike hissed. "It's Sad Face, and if you are feeling brave, I can always drop you off with your dino buddies." he sneered, curling his tentacles. The ship dove deeper into the dark ocean. On his screen, something huge appeared deep below. "There it is," Sad Face growled, his eyes fixed on his top hunter. The gigantic Mosasaurus turned and started chasing them. Sad Face quickly opened another portal and, with a powerful blast, transported the prehistoric legend back to ancient Egypt!

51 BC

KRAKOOM!

MEEEOOOW!!!

Winston couldn't believe his eyes as strange flying
creatures poured through the sparkly time portals.
A chilling thought then struck him...
They were about to witness
the destruction of Egypt!

"Ah-CHOOOOOOO!" Sad Face sneezed again, spraying octopus gunk all around the spaceship. Startled, Smokestrike jumped up and accidentally pressed the **Popcorn button,** several times as fluffy white popcorn exploded in all directions!

"**Nooo!**" Sad Face gasped as they lost control and slammed into the cat sphinx, knocking the statue's nose clean off. They then skidded to a halt right in front of Cleopatra's warriors and Winston, who were ready for battle.

"Another **PERFECT** situation!" Sad Face sloshed as he lunged through the popcorn, intent on blasting the Time Twister and sending Winston and Cleopatra's army back in time.

"Listen my brave warriors!" Cleopatra called out! "An alien has brought HUGE, stomping monsters to destroy Egypt! Winston our clever friend from the future, has a super plan! When that silly alien shoots his time beams at us, direct the blasts back to the dinosaurs. Send those creatures back to where they belong!" Winston squeezed his Cosmic Bone, for the first time ever his paws were shaking in fear! The giant dinosaurs were making the ground tremble.

Winston imagined giant shimmering traps, zooming out of the ground like magic, to contain the dangerous creatures. Suddenly a blinding white light burst from the Cosmic Bone, shooting across the desert in all directions. The light whizzed around the towering dinosaurs, folding into huge, futuristic cages. As Sad Face's scary time twisting blast flew through the air towards them!

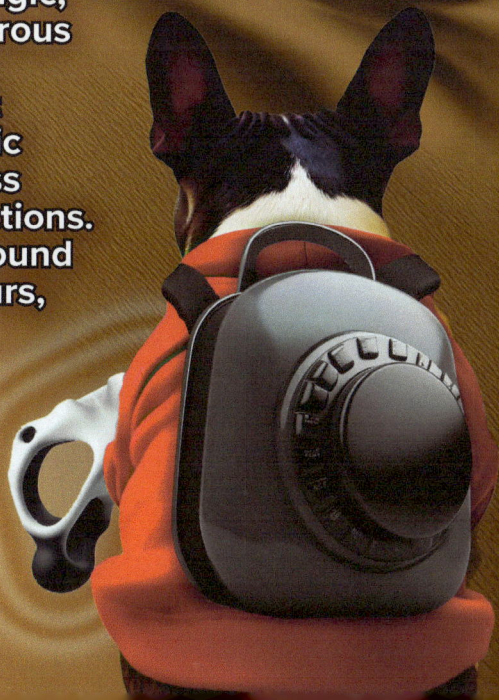

Cleopatra's army swiftly took cover, their polished shields flashing back the reflected beams. The concentrated energy shot right back towards the trapped dinosaurs, instantly hurtling them back to where they came from in distant past.

Sad Face bellowed in a mix of fury and humiliation as the disastrous scenes were now being broadcast intergalactically, and to top it off he had also missed out on the gigantic reptiles wreaking havoc across Egypt.

Pteranodons continued their destructive rampage across Egypt while the **Mosasaurus** tore through boats along the Nile River. Winston's stomach tightened, as Cleopatra's army was powerless against these immense creatures. With Sad Face and the time twister now gone from Ancient Egypt. Winston's options were running out quickly. His thoughts turned to Diesel and Teddy, his buddies that were left in the future in the tunnels underneath the bone shop on Slobberchops Lane. He hoped the orbs they discovered could help them stop Sad Face's evil plan.

"Thanks to you, Smokestrike...", Sad Face muttered. "My epic action series is now an intergalactic comedy show!" as he blasted another portal into the future. "It's now time to recruit a real demolition expert!"

"Well I will believe that when I see it," Smokestrike laughed.

"Oh, I'm quite certain you will..." Sad Face smirked as the portal burst open to unleash a colossal Kraken Octopus. One of Sad Face's long-lost incredibly destructive friends, whose immense size filled their entire field of vision.

KRAKEN

Back in the tunnels after everyone mysteriously vanished earlier in the story... Teddy and Diesel walked towards the floating orbs. Suddenly, a surge of raw energy washed over them, morphing their clothes into sleek, powerful super suits as they felt their new abilities awaken.

Teddy commanded the forces of fire, water, and light, while Diesel became the master of air, earth, and the ability to travel through time.

Diesel's eyes glowed as he muttered, "Totally Bonza, Mate! That mad ninja cat put our buddy in ancient Egypt with a bunch of rampaging dinosaurs! What a bonkers situation..."

"Dinosaurs in ancient Egypt..." Teddy replied. "Winston's going to need some serious backup, quickly... Let's go get him!"

FOUND HIM!

With a final, booming "**WOOF!**", Diesel activated the Realm Orb! The portal ripped open, pulling them both through time, with famous moments throughout history. On another great mission to save Winston, stop Sad Face and confront whatever prehistoric, intergalactic chaos lies ahead in the next thrilling adventure as **Superdogs!**

Spy Club Challenge

How many famous landmarks can you identify through time...

Leaning Tower of Pisa | Eiffel Tower | Chichen Itza | Colosseum | Pyramid of Giza | Great Wall of China | Parthenon | The Elizabeth Tower (Big Ben)

www.ingramcontent.com/pod-product-compliance
Lightning Source LLC
Chambersburg PA
CBHW041801040426
42448CB00001B/4